KEATON CAMPBELL

Fast Track Success: Become the Best

Contents

Chapter One: The Illusion of Complexity

L ife can be beautiful, or it can be challenging. It can be exhilarating or exhausting, joyful or painful. It's easy to get lost in the ups and downs of life, to feel like we're constantly struggling to keep up with the pace of the world around us. But what if we told you that life is actually much simpler than it seems?

In this book, we want to explore the idea that life is fundamentally simple, but we make it complicated with our emotions and overthinking. We believe that by understanding this concept, we can learn to navigate life with greater ease and clarity, and find more happiness and fulfillment along the way.

It's easy to get caught up in the complexities of modern life. We're bombarded with information from every direction, constantly stimulated by technology, and pressured to perform at our best in all areas of our lives. We often feel overwhelmed, stressed, and anxious as a result, and we struggle to find a sense of balance and purpose.

But what if we told you that all of this complexity is just an illusion? What if we said that life is actually quite simple, and that we create our own suffering by overthinking and getting lost in our emotions?

At its core, life is about survival and growth. We all have basic needs that must be met in order to survive, such as food, water, shelter, and safety. And once these needs are met, we naturally seek to grow and evolve as individuals. This can take many different forms, from personal relationships to creative pursuits to spiritual practices.

But somewhere along the way, we've added layers upon layers of complexity to our lives. We've developed complex social systems, intricate belief systems, and intricate ideas about our own identities and worth. We've created a never-ending cycle of desires and expectations that can never truly be fulfilled, leading to a constant sense of dissatisfaction and disappointment.

The truth is, life is simple. We eat when we're hungry, rest when we're tired, and seek out experiences that bring us joy and fulfillment. We connect with others, learn from our experiences, and grow and evolve over time. These are the basic building blocks of life, and everything else is just a layer of complexity that we've added on top.

So, if life is really so simple, why do we complicate it so much? In the chapters that follow, we'll explore the various ways in which we create complexity in our lives, and offer practical strategies for simplifying our lives and finding greater peace and happiness. By understanding the illusion of complexity, we can learn to navigate life with greater ease and clarity, and find more fulfillment and purpose along the way.

Chapter 2: Just Doing It

Have you ever had a dream, a goal, or a desire that you wanted to achieve, but felt stuck or overwhelmed by the steps it would take to get there? Maybe you've thought about starting a business, learning a new skill, or pursuing a passion project, but found yourself constantly delaying, procrastinating, or making excuses.

We've all been there. We've all had moments where we feel like we're stuck in a rut, unsure of how to move forward or make progress. But the truth is, if you want to do something, all you have to do is do it.

This may seem like an oversimplification, but it's the truth. The only thing standing between you and your goals is action. It's easy to get caught up in planning, strategizing, and thinking about all the ways things could go wrong. But the reality is that until you take action, nothing will ever change.

The power of taking action is immense. When you take action, you create momentum. You begin to build momentum towards your goal, and every step you take brings you closer to achieving it. The act of doing something, no matter how small, is always more powerful than thinking about doing something.

But taking action can be scary. It means stepping out of your comfort zone, taking risks, and facing the possibility of failure. It requires courage, determination, and a willingness to embrace uncertainty. But the rewards of taking action far outweigh the risks.

When you take action, you begin to build confidence in yourself. You start to believe that you can accomplish what you set out to do, and this belief fuels your motivation to keep going. You start to see progress, even if it's small, and this progress becomes a source of inspiration and motivation.

So how do you take action? It's simple. Just do it. Whatever it is that you want to achieve, take the first step. Don't overthink it, don't wait for the perfect moment, don't let fear hold you back. Just take action, no matter how small or insignificant it may seem.

If you want to start a business, take the first step by doing some research, reaching out to potential customers or partners, or creating a prototype. If you want to learn a new skill, start by taking a class, watching a tutorial, or practicing every day. If you want to pursue a passion project, start by setting aside some time each day or week to work on it.

The key is to break your goal down into small, manageable steps, and take action on each one. Every small action you take builds momentum, and over time, you'll find yourself making progress towards your goal.

Of course, taking action is easier said than done. It's easy to get caught up in our own doubts and fears, and to let procrastination or perfectionism get in the way. But the reality is that the only thing standing between you and your dreams is action.

So if you want to do something, all you have to do is do it. Take that first step, and keep taking action until you reach your goal. Don't wait for the perfect moment, or for someone else to give you permission. You have the power to make your dreams a reality, and all it takes is action.

Chapter 3: The Paralysis of Analysis

We've all been there. We want to do something, but we find ourselves overthinking the process. We analyze every possible scenario, consider every potential roadblock, and weigh the pros and cons of each action. In some cases, we even create elaborate plans and strategies to achieve our goals.

While there's nothing wrong with being prepared and thinking things through, the problem with overthinking is that it often leads to analysis paralysis. We become so consumed with the details and possibilities that we fail to take any action at all. We find more reasons not to do something than to do it, and in the end, we're left feeling frustrated and unfulfilled.

The truth is, overthinking is a trap. It's easy to get caught up in our own thoughts and doubts, and to let fear and uncertainty hold us back. But the reality is that most of the time, what we want we don't have for a reason. Maybe we're not ready for it yet, or maybe it's not really what we need. Whatever the reason, overthinking and analysis paralysis only serve to delay our progress and prevent us from living the life we want.

If you want to achieve something, you need to take action. You need to be willing to make mistakes, take risks, and learn from failure. You need to trust your intuition and have faith in yourself. Overthinking only leads to doubt, fear, and indecision.

The problem with overthinking is that it creates a sense of false control. We believe that by analyzing every possibility, we can avoid failure and ensure success. But the reality is that life is unpredictable, and there's no way to guarantee outcomes. The only way to truly succeed is to take action and learn from our mistakes along the way.

Another problem with overthinking is that it often leads to self-doubt and negative self-talk. We begin to question our abilities and worth, and to focus on all the reasons why we can't achieve our goals. This negative mindset only serves to reinforce our fears and prevent us from taking action.

To overcome overthinking, you need to develop a mindset of action. You need to focus on what you can control, and take small, deliberate steps towards your goals. You need to embrace uncertainty, and be willing to adapt and change course as needed. Most importantly, you need to let go of the need for perfect outcomes, and be willing to learn from your mistakes.

If you find yourself overthinking, try taking a step back and focusing on your intentions. What do you really want? Why do you want it? What's holding you back? Once you have clarity on your intentions, take action. Start with small steps, and build momentum over time. Remember that progress, not perfection, is the key to success.

In conclusion, overthinking and analysis paralysis only serve to delay our progress and prevent us from living the life we want. If you want to achieve something, you need to take action and learn from your mistakes along the way. Let go of the need for perfect outcomes, and focus on progress over perfection. Trust yourself, trust the process, and have faith that you can achieve anything you set your mind to.

Chapter 4: Knowledge is Power

In today's fast-paced world, knowledge is power. The more we know, the more we can accomplish, and the more successful we can be. But, how do we acquire knowledge? How do we know what to learn and where to find it?

The truth is, knowledge is not something that just falls into our laps. We have to actively seek it out. We have to be willing to learn, to grow, and to expand our horizons. If we want to achieve our goals and fulfill our potential, we have to be willing to invest time and effort into acquiring the knowledge and skills we need.

So, where do we start? The first step is to identify what we need to learn. What skills do we need to acquire to achieve our goals? What knowledge do we need to succeed in our chosen field? Once we have identified our areas of focus, we can start to explore different avenues for acquiring knowledge.

One of the most obvious ways to acquire knowledge is through formal education. Whether it's pursuing a degree, attending a workshop or seminar, or taking an online course, formal education can provide us with the structured learning environment and the guidance we need to acquire new skills and knowledge.

However, formal education is not the only way to acquire knowledge. We can also learn from books, podcasts, documentaries, and other media. We can seek out mentors and experts in our field, and learn from their experience and wisdom. We can attend conferences and networking events, and connect with others who share our interests and passions.

But, it's important to remember that not all sources of knowledge are created equal. We need to be discerning about where we seek information and who we learn from. For example, if we want to learn how to be a doctor, we wouldn't go to a construction worker for advice. Similarly, if we want to learn how to drive a truck, we wouldn't ask a desk jockey for guidance.

We need to be intentional about seeking out knowledge from credible sources, and from those who have the experience and expertise to guide us. We need to be willing to invest time and effort into our own learning, and to be open to new ideas and perspectives.

The reality is, we can't find something unless we're looking for it. If we want to acquire knowledge and skills, we have to be intentional about seeking them out. We have to be willing to invest time and effort into our own learning, and to be open to new ideas and perspectives.

In conclusion, knowledge is power, but we have to actively seek it out. We have to be intentional about identifying what we need to learn, and where we can find the information and guidance we need. We have to be discerning about the sources of knowledge we rely on, and be willing to invest time and effort into our own learning. If we're willing to do the work, we can acquire the knowledge and skills we need to achieve our goals and fulfill our potential.

Chapter 5: Good is Not Good Enough

Many of us settle for a good life. We have a good job, a good home, good relationships, and good health. We're comfortable and content, but is that really enough? Can't we strive for something more? Can't we aim for the best?

The reality is, settling for good is not good enough. We should always aim for better, for the best. There is always room for improvement in every aspect of our lives. Whether it's in our career, our relationships, our health, or our personal development, there is always something we can do to make things better.

When we settle for good, we limit ourselves. We limit our potential and our ability to achieve great things. We become complacent and stagnant, and we stop growing and evolving. We may be comfortable, but we're not truly happy or fulfilled.

So, how do we aim for the best? How do we push ourselves to be better in every aspect of our lives? The first step is to identify what we want. What are our goals and aspirations? What do we want to achieve in our lives?

Once we have identified our goals, we can start to explore different ways to achieve them. We can set SMART (specific, measurable, achievable, relevant, and time-bound) goals and develop a plan to achieve them. We can seek out mentors and experts in our field and learn from their experience and expertise. We can take risks and try new things, even if they make us feel uncomfortable or uncertain.

But, it's important to remember that aiming for the best doesn't mean striving for perfection. We will never be perfect, and that's okay. We will always have room for improvement, and that's what makes life exciting and fulfilling. We should strive to be the best version of ourselves, but we should also be kind and compassionate to ourselves when we fall short.

Aiming for the best applies to every aspect of our lives, from our personal development to our relationships to our careers. We should aim for the best relationships, the best health, the best career, and the best personal development. We should constantly be pushing ourselves to grow and evolve, and to be the best we can be.

In conclusion, settling for good is not good enough. We should always aim for better, for the best. There is always room for improvement in every aspect of our lives, and we should constantly be pushing ourselves to be the best we can be. Aiming for the best doesn't mean striving for perfection, but rather striving to be the best version of ourselves. We should always be growing and evolving, and never settle for anything less than the best.

Chapter 6: Your Mindset Matters

Your mindset is a powerful tool that can either limit or empower you. The way you think and perceive the world around you can have a significant impact on your life. If you have a negative mindset, you are more likely to see obstacles and problems in every situation. On the other hand, if you have a positive mindset, you are more likely to see opportunities and possibilities.

It's important to understand that your mindset determines your reality. If you believe that something is impossible, it becomes impossible for you. But if you believe that something is possible, you are more likely to find a way to make it happen. Your thoughts and beliefs shape your perception of the world, and they can have a profound impact on your actions and outcomes.

One way to understand how your mindset works is to think about the concept of selective attention. When you focus your attention on something, you start to see it everywhere. For example, if you're thinking about buying a new car and you have your eye on a particular make and model, you start to see that car everywhere you go. You might see it on the road, in car commercials, or even in parking lots. It seems like everyone is driving that car. This is because your mind is selectively filtering out other information and focusing on the things that align with your current thinking.

The same principle applies to your mindset. If you have a negative mindset, you will start to see negative things everywhere you go. You will see problems and obstacles in every situation, and you will find it difficult to see the good in anything. But if you have a positive mindset, you will start to see opportunities and possibilities everywhere you go. You will see the good in every situation, and you will find it easier to overcome challenges and obstacles.

It's important to understand that you have the power to control your mindset. You can choose to focus on the positive or the negative in any situation. You can choose to look for opportunities or problems. You can choose to see the good or the bad in people. Your mindset is entirely within your control, and it's up to you to choose how you want to perceive the world.

If you want to change your mindset, it's important to start by changing your thoughts and beliefs. You can do this by practicing positive affirmations, visualizing positive outcomes, and focusing on the good in every situation. You can also surround yourself with positive people and consume positive content that uplifts and inspires you.

In conclusion, your mindset matters. The way you think and perceive the world around you can have a significant impact on your life. Your mindset determines your reality, and you have the power to control it. If you want to achieve great things in life, you need to start by adopting a positive mindset. By focusing on the good and the opportunities, you will find them in abundance. So, choose to see the good in every situation, and watch your life transform in amazing ways.

Chapter 7: Starting Small to Make Big Changes

We all have something we want to improve or achieve in life, but sometimes the thought of taking on such a monumental task can be daunting. We might not know where to begin, what steps to take, or even what resources we need to make it happen. It can be overwhelming, and that's why many people give up before they even start.

But here's the truth: the most significant changes in our lives often start with the smallest, simplest steps. Taking action, even if it seems small or insignificant, can be the key to making progress toward your goals.

Let's say you want to start a new exercise routine, but you're not sure where to start. The thought of joining a gym and figuring out how to use all the equipment might seem intimidating. Instead, start with the simplest exercises that require no equipment: pushups, sit-ups, and squats. Do them every day, and you'll be amazed at how quickly your body starts to change.

The same principle applies to any area of your life. If you're not doing anything to move forward, you're going nowhere. But if you take even the smallest step, you're making progress. And progress, no matter how small, is better than standing still.

Think about it this way: if you're driving a car and you want to get to a destination that's 100 miles away, you don't start by thinking about the entire journey. You focus on the first step: getting in the car and starting the engine. Then you focus on the next step: driving out of your driveway. Before you know it, you're on the highway and making progress toward your goal.

It's the same with any goal or task. Break it down into the smallest, simplest steps, and focus on taking action one step at a time. Before you know it, you'll be making progress, building momentum, and achieving things you never thought possible.

Remember, the key to starting small is to do something, anything, to move forward. Don't worry about perfection or taking the perfect step. Just take action, and you'll be on your way to making big changes in your life.

Chapter 8: Embrace Failure as a Learning Opportunity

W e often fear failure because we see it as a sign of weakness or incompetence. But the truth is, failure is an inevitable part of the journey to success. If you're not failing, you're not trying hard enough or taking enough risks.

Instead of fearing failure, embrace it as a learning opportunity. Every time you fail, you have the chance to learn from your mistakes and grow. The key is to approach failure with a growth mindset, rather than a fixed one.

A fixed mindset believes that your abilities and intelligence are static, and that failure is a reflection of your inherent shortcomings. In contrast, a growth mindset believes that your abilities and intelligence can be developed through hard work and perseverance, and that failure is an opportunity for growth and learning.

To adopt a growth mindset, start reframing your failures as opportunities to learn and improve. Analyze what went wrong and identify areas where you can improve. Then, make a plan to address those areas and try again.

It's also important to remember that failure is not a reflection of your worth as a person. Everyone fails at some point in their lives, and it's how we respond to failure that defines us.

So, don't be afraid to take risks and make mistakes. Embrace failure as a necessary step on the path to success, and use it as a tool for growth and self-improvement.

We live in a world where success is often measured by how much we achieve, and failures are seen as setbacks that hold us back. But what if we told you that the most successful people in the world see failures as lessons, and that the only way to truly fail is to learn nothing from your mistakes?

The truth is that failure is not the opposite of success – it's a necessary part of the journey towards success. Every time you fail, you have the opportunity to learn something new, to develop new skills and to grow as a person.

Successful people understand this. They don't see failures as obstacles or signs of weakness, but as opportunities to learn and improve. They analyze their mistakes, identify areas for improvement, and then use that knowledge to make better decisions in the future.

The key to turning failure into a learning opportunity is to adopt a growth mindset. This means viewing challenges as opportunities for growth, and seeing failures as a natural part of the learning process. It's about recognizing that your abilities and intelligence are not fixed, but can be developed through hard work and dedication.

When you fail, it's easy to feel discouraged and to give up. But the most successful people in the world understand that failure is not the end – it's just the beginning. They use failure as a tool for self-improvement, and they keep pushing forward until they achieve their goals.

So, the next time you experience a setback or a failure, remember that you have a choice. You can choose to see it as a defeat, or you can choose to see it as an opportunity to learn and grow. The choice is yours, and it will ultimately determine whether you succeed or fail in life.

Chapter 9: The Gratitude Attitude

Have you ever stopped to think about all the good things in your life? The things you take for granted, like your health, your loved ones, or your job. How often do you stop to appreciate them and give thanks for them? If you're like most people, you probably don't do it enough. In fact, you may even focus more on what you don't have than on what you do have.

But what if I told you that cultivating an attitude of gratitude could transform your life? It may sound cliché, but it's true. Gratitude is one of the most powerful emotions you can feel. It has the power to change your perspective, your mood, and your behavior.

When you focus on what you're grateful for, you're acknowledging the good in your life. You're shifting your attention away from what's lacking and toward what's present. This mindset can help you to feel more positive, optimistic, and fulfilled. It can also help you to attract more good things into your life.

But it's not just about feeling good. Practicing gratitude can have a real impact on your success. When you're grateful for what you have, you're more likely to take care of it and make the most of it. You're also more likely to take risks and pursue opportunities because you believe you have something to build on.

On the other hand, when you're constantly focused on what you don't have, you're more likely to feel discouraged and overwhelmed. You may feel like you don't have what it takes to succeed, or that you'll never be happy until you have more. This negative mindset can hold you back and keep you stuck.

So how do you cultivate an attitude of gratitude? It's simple, but it takes practice. Start by making a conscious effort to focus on the good in your life. Take time each day to reflect on what you're grateful for, whether it's a loving relationship, a roof over your head, or a good meal. Write it down if you can, and savor the feeling of gratitude.

Another way to cultivate gratitude is to give back. When you help others, you not only make a positive impact on their lives, but you also feel good about yourself. Volunteer your time or donate to a cause you care about. You'll be surprised at how good it feels to make a difference.

Finally, remember to be grateful for the journey, not just the destination. It's easy to focus solely on the end result and forget about all the steps it took to get there. But every step along the way is an opportunity for growth, learning, and gratitude. Be thankful for the progress you're making, even if it's slow, and trust that it's leading you to where you want to go.

In conclusion, gratitude is a powerful emotion that can transform your life and your success. By focusing on the good in your life, giving back, and being grateful for the journey, you can cultivate an attitude of gratitude that will serve you well in all areas of your life. So take a moment right now to appreciate all the good in your life, and watch as it multiplies.

Chapter 10: The Cost of Wasted Time

Time is our most valuable and finite resource, yet we often take it for granted. We waste precious minutes, hours, and even days on mindless activities, procrastination, and distractions that bring us no closer to our goals. We convince ourselves that we'll get to the important things eventually, but the truth is that wasted time is a cost we can never get back.

Think about how much time you spend scrolling through social media, watching TV, or playing video games. Think about the times when you said you would start working on that important project, but instead, you found yourself distracted by something else. These moments might seem harmless, but they add up.

In a day, we have 24 hours or 1,440 minutes to work with. If we spend just 2 hours a day scrolling through social media, that's 14 hours a week or 728 hours a year. That's almost a month of wasted time every year. Imagine what you could accomplish with an extra month of focused effort towards your goals.

Now, consider the opportunity cost of wasted time. Every moment you spend doing something unproductive is a moment you could be using to improve yourself, build your skills, or work towards your goals. You could be reading a book, learning a new language, or practicing a new skill. Instead, you're choosing to waste your time on activities that don't contribute to your growth.

19

The worst part is that wasted time doesn't just cost us in terms of lost productivity. It also has a psychological impact. When we waste time, we feel guilty, stressed, and anxious. We know we're not making progress, and that feeling can weigh on us heavily.

But, the good news is that wasted time is a habit that can be broken. Start by identifying the activities that are consuming your time without providing any real value. Then, create a plan to reduce or eliminate those activities. Set specific goals for what you want to accomplish each day and hold yourself accountable.

Next, prioritize your time. Identify the tasks that are most important to you and focus your energy on them. Create a schedule that allows you to make progress towards your goals every day.

Finally, remember that time is a gift, and it's up to us to use it wisely. Make the most of every moment by being intentional about how you spend your time. Don't let wasted time be the cost of your inaction. Take control of your time and use it to create the life you want.

Chapter 11: The Hidden Key to Success

E fficiency is key to making the most of your time and achieving your goals. When you are efficient, you can get more done in less time, leaving you with more time to focus on other important tasks or activities. In this chapter, we will discuss the importance of efficiency in our lives, and how to be more efficient in everything we do.

Firstly, being efficient means doing things in the most effective way possible. This can involve using tools, technology, or systems that help us complete tasks more quickly and accurately. It can also involve focusing on the most important tasks and prioritizing them, so that we can complete them first and move on to other tasks.

One of the most important reasons to be efficient is that it helps us to save time. Time is one of the most valuable resources we have, and it is a finite resource. We cannot make more time, so it is important to make the most of the time we have. Being efficient allows us to get more done in less time, so that we can use the time we save to focus on other important things.

Another reason to be efficient is that it can help us to reduce stress and anxiety. When we have a lot of tasks to complete, or when we are feeling overwhelmed by the amount of work we have to do, it can be easy to become stressed or anxious. By being efficient and completing tasks more quickly and accurately, we can reduce the amount of stress and anxiety we experience, which can lead to a more relaxed and productive state of mind.

Efficiency can also help us to achieve our goals more quickly and effectively. When we are able to complete tasks more quickly and accurately, we can make progress towards our goals more quickly. This can be especially important when we are working towards long-term goals, such as starting a new business or learning a new skill.

To be more efficient, it is important to focus on the most important tasks first. This means prioritizing tasks based on their importance and urgency, and completing the most important tasks first. It is also important to eliminate distractions and focus on the task at hand. This might involve turning off your phone or email notifications, or finding a quiet place to work where you can focus on the task at hand.

Another way to be more efficient is to use tools and technology that can help us complete tasks more quickly and accurately. This might involve using project management software to keep track of tasks and deadlines, or using a time-tracking tool to help you stay on track and make the most of your time.

In conclusion, efficiency is a crucial component of success in all areas of life. By being efficient, we can save time, reduce stress and anxiety, and achieve our goals more quickly and effectively. To be more efficient, it is important to focus on the most important tasks first, eliminate distractions, and use tools and technology to help us complete tasks more quickly and accurately.

Efficiency truly is key to success. It's the difference between just getting by and thriving in all aspects of life. As mentioned before, it's not just about working harder, but working smarter. And the smartest way to work is by being efficient.

Think about it this way - if you can accomplish the same amount of work in half the time, you essentially just doubled your productivity. That means you have more time to focus on other things, like learning new skills, spending time with loved ones, or even just taking a break to recharge your batteries.

But it's not just about getting things done quickly. Efficiency is also about doing things in the most effective way possible. That means finding ways to streamline processes, eliminating unnecessary steps, and maximizing output while minimizing input.

For example, if you're running a business, you might find that automating certain tasks can save you time and money. Or, if you're studying for an exam, you might find that taking frequent breaks and using a study method that works for you can help you retain information more efficiently.

Efficiency is also about prioritizing your time and energy. Instead of spreading yourself thin trying to do everything at once, focus on the tasks that will have the biggest impact on your goals. That means setting clear priorities, delegating tasks to others when possible, and saying no to things that don't align with your values or goals.

Ultimately, being efficient is about working smarter, not harder. It's about finding ways to get more done in less time, while also improving the quality of your work and your life. By making efficiency a priority in everything you do, you'll be on your way to success in no time.

Chapter 12: Conclusion

It has been quite a journey, and I hope you have gained a lot of value from this book. We've covered a lot of ground, from the importance of taking action, not overthinking, learning and finding what we need, not settling for good enough, controlling our mindset, gratitude, and efficiency.

Now, I want to leave you with some final words of motivation. The reality is that life is short, and time is precious. We can't afford to waste it on things that don't matter, or that don't help us achieve our goals and dreams. It's time to stop making excuses and start taking action, no matter how small the steps may seem.

You have the power to shape your life into something amazing, but it starts with a mindset shift. Believe in yourself, and know that you have what it takes to achieve your dreams. You must take responsibility for your life and your decisions, and never settle for less than what you deserve.

Success is not easy, but it is achievable. It requires hard work, dedication, and a never-give-up attitude. Failure is not the end, but rather a lesson that we can learn from to help us succeed in the future.

Remember, success is not just about making money or achieving fame. It's about living a fulfilling and purposeful life, one where you are happy and satisfied with the person you have become.

In conclusion, I want to encourage you to take action, believe in yourself, be grateful, and work efficiently towards your goals. Life is too short to waste on anything less than your best, so go out there and make your dreams a reality. Thank you for reading, and I wish you all the best in your journey to success.